Easy Keto Vegetarian Cookbook

Easy and Delicious Low-Carb, Plant-Based Recipes to Lose Weight and Feel Great

Lidia Wong

TABLE OF CONTENTS

INTRODUCTION

The keto diet is the shortened term for ketogenic diet and it is essentially a high-fat and low-carb diet that helps you lose weight, thereby bringing various health benefits. This diet drastically restricts your carb intake while increasing your fat intake; this pushes your body to go into a state know as "*ketosis*". We will tackle ketosis in a bit.

The human body uses glucose from carbs to fuel metabolic pathways—meaning various bodily functions like digestion, breathing, etc.. Essentially, anything that needs energy. Even when you are resting, the body needs fuel or energy for you to continue living. If you think about it, when have you ever stopped breathing, or your heart stopped beating, or your liver stopped from cleansing the body, or your kidneys from filtering blood?

Never, unless you're dead, which is the only time in which the body doesn't need energy. In normal circumstances, glucose is the primary pathway when it comes to sourcing the body's energy.

But the body also has another pathway; it can utilize fats to fuel the various bodily processes. And this is what we call "*ketosis*". And the body can only enter ketosis when there is no glucose available, thus the reason for sticking to a low-carb diet is essential in the keto diet. Since no glucose is available, the body is pushed to use fats—it can either come from the food you consume or from your body's fat reserves—the adipose tissue or from the flabby parts of your body. This is how the keto diet helps you lose weight, by burning up all those stored fats that you have and using it to fuel bodily processes.

That said, if for whatever reason you are a vegetarian, following a ketogenic diet can be extremely difficult. A vegetarian diet is largely free of animal products, which means that food tends to be usually high in carbohydrates. Still, with careful planning, it is possible. This Cookbook will provide you with various easy and delicious dishes to help you stick to your ketogenic diet plan while being a vegetarian.

Enjoy!

Spicy Bowls

Preparation time: 10 minutes

Cooking time: 15 minutes

Servings: 4

Ingredients:

- 1 cup baby spinach
- ½ cup cherry tomatoes, halved
- ¼ teaspoon cardamom, ground

- 1 teaspoon turmeric powder
- 1 tablespoon olive oil
- ½ cup coconut cream
- ½ cup green olives, pitted and halved
- A pinch of salt and black pepper
- ½ cup cucumbers, sliced
- 1 tablespoon parsley, chopped

Directions:

1. Heat up a pan with the oil over medium heat, add the olives and the tomatoes, toss and cook for 5 minutes.
2. Add the spinach and the other ingredients, toss, cook over medium heat for 10 minutes, divide into bowls and serve.

Nutrition:

calories 116, fat 11.3, fiber 1.6, carbs 4.2, protein 1.3

Baked Cheesy Artichokes

Preparation time: 10 minutes

Cooking time: 45 minutes

Servings: 6

Ingredients:

- 12 ounces canned artichokes, halved
- 1 cup spinach, chopped
- 1 cup almond milk
- 2 garlic cloves, minced

- 1 tablespoon dill, chopped
- ½ cup cashew cheese, shredded
- A pinch of salt and black pepper
- teaspoons olive oil

Directions:

1. Heat up a pan with the oil over medium heat, add the garlic, artichokes, salt and pepper, stir and cook for 5 minutes.
2. Transfer this to a baking dish, add the spinach, almond milk and the other ingredients, toss a bit, bake at 380 degrees F for 40 minutes, divide between plates and serve for breakfast.

Nutrition:

calories 149, fat 12.2, fiber 4.3, carbs 9.7, protein 3.5

Creamy Coconut-Sesame Bread

Preparation Time: 10 minutes

Cooking Time: 30 minutes

Serving: 4

Ingredients:

- 4 tbsp flax seed powder + 1 ½ cups water
- 1 cup coconut flour
- 2/3 cup cream cheese
- 4 tbsp sesame oil + extra for brushing
- 1 tsp baking powder
- 2 tbsp psyllium husk powder
- 1 tsp salt
- 1 tbsp sesame seeds

Directions:

1. Preheat the oven to 400 °F.
2. In a medium bowl, mix the flax seed powder with water and allow soaking for 5 minutes.
3. Whisk in the cream cheese and sesame oil until well mixed.

4. Mix in the coconut flour, psyllium husk powder, salt, and baking powder until adequately combined.
5. Grease a 9 x 5 inches baking tray with cooking spray and spread the dough in the tray. Allow the mixture to stand for 5 minutes and then brush with some sesame oil.
6. Sprinkle the sesame seeds on top and bake the dough for 30 minutes or until golden brown on top and set within.
7. Take out the bread and allow cooling for a few minutes. Slice and serve for breakfast.

Nutrition:

Calories: 263, Total Fat: 26.4g, Saturated Fat: 8.8g, Total Carbs: 4 g, Dietary Fiber: 1g, Sugar: 3g, Protein:4 g, Sodium: 826mg

Baked Bok Choy and Tomatoes

Preparation time: 10 minutes

Cooking time: 30 minutes

Servings: 4

Ingredients:

- ½ pound cherry tomatoes, halved
- 1 pound bok choy, torn
- 2 tablespoons olive oil
- 2 teaspoons rosemary, dried
- 1 teaspoon cloves, ground
- ½ teaspoon nutmeg, ground
- 1 teaspoon coriander, ground
- 2 tablespoons balsamic vinegar

Directions:

1. In a roasting pan, combine the bok choy with the cherry tomatoes and the other ingredients, toss and bake at 400 degrees F for 30 minutes,
2. Divide everything between plates and serve.

Nutrition:

calories 220, fat 2, fiber 4, carbs 6, protein 10

Radish Hash Browns

Preparation Time: 10 minutes

Cooking Time: 10 minutes

Servings: 4

Ingredients:

- 2 shallots, peeled, sliced
- ¼ teaspoon paprika
- ¼ teaspoon thyme

- 1 organic egg
- 1 tablespoon coconut flour
- 2-ounces cheddar cheese
- 1 lb. radishes, shredded
- ¼ teaspoon pepper
- ¼ teaspoon sea salt

Directions:

1. Add ingredients into a mixing bowl, except for the butter and mix well. Melt the butter in a pan over medium heat. Add a scoop of mixture into the pan and fry until lightly browned on both sides. Serve and enjoy!

Nutritional Values (Per Serving):

Calories: 176 Fat: 10.4 g Carbohydrates: 13 g Sugar: 4 g Cholesterol: 116 mg Protein: 7.9 g

Mashed Turnips

Preparation Time: 5 minutes

Cooking Time: 20 minutes

Servings: 4

Ingredients:

- 3 cups turnip, diced
- 2 garlic cloves, minced
- 3 tablespoons butter, melted
- ¼ cup heavy cream
- Pepper and salt to taste

Directions:

1. Bring your turnip to a boil in a saucepan over medium heat. Cook for about 20 minutes, then drain turnips and mash until smooth. Add butter, garlic, heavy cream, pepper, and salt. Mix well. Serve warm and enjoy!

Nutritional Values (Per Serving):

Calories: 132 Cholesterol: 33 mg Protein: 1.2 g
Carbohydrates: 7 g Fat: 11.5 g

Creamy Coconut Curry

Preparation Time: 15 minutes

Cooking Time: 30 minutes

Servings: 4

Ingredients:

- ¼ of an onion, sliced
- 1 teaspoon garlic, minced
- 1 teaspoon ginger, minced
- 1 tablespoon red curry paste

- 2 teaspoons soy sauce
- 1 cup broccoli florets
- 1 handful spinach
- ½ cup coconut cream
- 4 tablespoons coconut oil

Directions:

1. In a saucepan over medium-high heat, heat your coconut oil. Add your onion to the pan and cook until softened. Add garlic and cook until lightly browned. Reduce heat to medium-low, adding broccoli, stir well. Cook for about 20 minutes, then add the curry paste and stir. Add spinach over broccoli and cook until wilted. Add soy sauce, ginger and coconut cream, and stir. Simmer for an additional 10 minutes. Serve hot and enjoy!

Nutritional Values (Per Serving):

Calories: 235 Cholesterol: 0 mg Sugar: 2.1 g
Carbohydrates: 8.4 g Fat: 22.3 g Protein: 4.1 g

Cheesy Grits

Preparation Time: 5 minutes

Cooking Time: 8 minutes

Servings: 4

Ingredients:

- ½ cup butter, unsalted
- ½ cup vegetable broth

- 8 eggs, organic
- ½ cup cheddar cheese, shredded
- 1 teaspoon sea salt

Directions:

1. In a mixing bowl add your eggs, broth, and sea salt, mix well. Melt butter in a pan over medium heat. Place your egg mixture into the pan and cook for 8 minutes or until the mixture thickens and curds form. Add the cheese to the pan and stir well. Remove the pan from heat. Serve warm and enjoy!

Nutritional Values (Per Serving):

Calories: 388 Cholesterol: 403 mg Sugar: 0.9 g Fat: 36.5 g Carbohydrates: 1.4 g Protein: 14.8 g

Avocado Pesto Zoodles

Preparation time: 10 minutes

Cooking time: 10 minutes

Servings: 2

Ingredients:

- 4 medium zucchini, spiralized
- 2 avocados, halved
- 1 tablespoon pine nuts
- ½ cup fresh basil
- 2 teaspoons olive oil
- 1 tablespoon minced garlic
- 4 tablespoons shredded Parmesan cheese
- ½ teaspoon salt
- ½ teaspoon freshly ground black pepper

Directions:

1. In the bowl of a food processor, combine the avocados, pine nuts, and basil. Pulse until a paste forms, using a few tablespoons of water to thin the consistency if necessary.

2. Heat a medium skillet over medium-high heat and pour in the olive oil. Add the zoodles and garlic and sauté for 5 to 7 minutes.
3. Add the avocado pesto to the skillet and stir until well combined.
4. Cook for an additional 1 to 2 minutes and top with the Parmesan cheese, salt, and pepper.

Nutrition:

calories 404, fat, 31g, protein 14g, carbs 27g, fiber 14g, sugar 7g, sodium 766mg

Roasted Squash

Preparation Time: 10 minutes

Cooking Time: 1 hour

Servings: 3

Ingredients:

- 2 lbs. summer squash, cut into 1-inch pieces
- 1/8 tsp pepper
- 1/8 tsp garlic powder

- 1 large lemon juice
- 3 tbsp olive oil
- 1/8 tsp paprika
- Pepper
- Salt

Directions:

1. Preheat the oven to 400 F/ 204 C.
2. Spray a baking tray with cooking spray.
3. Place squash pieces onto the prepared baking tray and drizzle with olive oil.
4. Season with paprika, pepper, and garlic powder.
5. Squeeze lemon juice over the squash and bake in preheated oven for 50-60 minutes.
6. Serve hot and enjoy.

Nutritions:

Calories 182 Fat 15 g Carbohydrates 12.3 g Sugar 11 g Protein 3.2 g Cholesterol 0 mg

Celery Salad

Preparation Time: 10 minutes

Cooking Time: 0 minutes

Servings: 6

Ingredients:

- 6 cups celery, sliced
- ¼ tsp celery seed
- 1 tbsp olive oil
- 1 tbsp lemon juice
- 2 tsp lemon zest, grated
- 1 tbsp parsley, chopped
- Sea salt

Directions:

1. Add all ingredients into the large mixing bowl and toss well.
2. Serve immediately and enjoy.

Nutritions: :

Calories 38 Fat 2.5 g Carbohydrates 3.3 g Sugar 1.5 g Protein 0.8 g Cholesterol 0 mg

Mozzarella Cheese (vegan)

Preparation time: 20 minutes

Cooking time: 0 minute

Servings: 16

Ingredients:

- 1 cup raw cashews (unsalted)
- ½ cup macadamia nuts (unsalted)
- ½ cup pine nuts
- ½ tbsp. coconut oil
- ½ tsp. light miso paste
- 2 tbsp. agar-agar
- 1 tsp. fresh lime juice
- ½ cup water
- 1 tsp. Himalayan salt

Directions:

1. Cover the cashews with water in a small bowl and let sit for 4 to 6 hours. Rinse and drain the cashews after soaking. Make sure no water is left.
2. Mix the agar-agar with the ½ cup of water in a

small saucepan. Put the pan over medium heat.

3. Bring the agar-agar mixture to a boil. After 1 minute, take it off the heat and set the mixture aside to cool down.
4. Put all the other ingredients—except the coconut oil—in a blender or food processor. Blend until everything is well combined.
5. Add the agar-agar with water and blend again until all ingredients have been fully incorporated.
6. Grease a medium-sized bowl with the coconut oil to prevent the cheese from sticking to the edges. Gently transfer the cheese mixture into the bowl by using a spatula.
7. Refrigerate the bowl, uncovered, for about 3 hours until the cheese is firm; then serve and enjoy!
8. Alternatively, store the cheese in an airtight container in the fridge. Consume within 6 days. Store for a maximum of 60 days in the freezer and thaw at room temperature.

Nutritions:

Calories: 101kcal, Net Carbs: 2.1g, Fat: 9.2g, Protein: 2.2g, Fiber: 0.9g, Sugar: 0.9g

Cheesy Crustless Quiche

Preparation Time: 30 minutes

Cooking Time: 1 hour

Servings: 6

Ingredients:

- 6 small Roma tomatoes
- 6 large eggs, beaten
- 1 cup cottage cheese
- ½ cup thinly sliced green onion

- ¼ teaspoon Italian Herb Blend
- ½ teaspoon Spike Seasoning (optional but recommended)
- ½ cup half and half
- 2 cups shredded Swiss cheese
- ¼ cup finely grated Parmesan cheese
- ¼ cup thinly sliced basil
- Salt and fresh-ground black pepper to taste

Directions:

1. Preheat oven to 350 °F. Coat a 9-10" glass or crockery pie dish with non-stick spray.
2. Cut 3 small Roma tomatoes in half lengthwise and scoop out the seeds. Pat the interior dry with paper towels and then chop the tomatoes.
3. Break the eggs into a large bowl, add the half and half, Italian Herb Blend, Spike Seasonings, salt and pepper. Whisk until combined.
4. Stir in the cottage cheese, Swiss cheese, Parmesan cheese, chopped tomatoes, and green onion.
5. Pour into the prepared pie dish and bake for 30 minutes.

6. Meanwhile, thinly slice 3 remaining small Roma tomatoes and put on a plate between paper towel layers. Gently press to help draw out the moisture.
7. After 30 minutes, remove the quiche from the oven and distribute sliced tomatoes and sliced basil on top of the quiche.
8. Return to oven and bake an additional 30 minutes or slightly more if the center doesn't seem set enough.
9. Turn oven to Broil and cook for a minute or two until browned. But keep a close eye on it so the basil does not burn.
10. Allow the quiche to sit for 5-10 minutes before cutting.
11. Serve warm or at room temperature.

Nutritions:

Calories: 301, Total Fats: 20g, Carbohydrates: 8g, Fiber: 1g, Protein: 23g, Sugar: 4g

Roasted Broccoli with Almonds

Preparation Time: 12 minutes

Cooking Time: 20 minutes

Servings: 4

Ingredients:

- 1 ½ lbs. broccoli, cut into florets
- 1 tablespoon lemon juice
- 3 tablespoons olive oil

- 3 tablespoons almonds, slivered, toasted
- 2 garlic cloves, sliced
- ¼ teaspoon pepper
- ¼ teaspoon sea salt
- ¼ cup cheese, grated

Directions:

1. Preheat your oven to 425°Fahrenheit. Spray baking dish with cooking spray. Add broccoli, garlic, oil, pepper, and salt in a mixing bowl and toss well. Spread the broccoli in the prepared baking dish and roast in preheated oven for 20 minutes. Add lemon juice, grated cheese, almonds over broccoli, toss well. Serve hot and enjoy!

Nutritional Values (Per Serving):

Calories: 206 Fat: 15.7 g Sugar: 3.2 g Carbohydrates: 13 g Cholesterol: 7 mg Protein: 7.6 g

Homemade Vegan Sausages

Preparation Time: 10 minutes

Cooking Time: 15 minutes

Serves: 4

Ingredients:

- 1 cup Vital Wheat Gluten
- ¼ cup Walnuts
- ¼ cup Minced Onion
- 1 tbsp Minced Garlic
- 1 tsp Smoked Paprika
- 1 tsp Cumin Powder
- ½ tsp Dried Marjoram
- ¼ tsp Dried Oregano
- ¼ tsp Salt
- ¼ tsp Pepper
- ¼ cup Water
- 2 tbsp Olive Oil

Directions:

1. Heat olive oil in a pan. Sautee onions and garlic until soft.
2. Add onions and garlic together with the rest of the ingredients in a food processor. Pulse into a homogenous texture.
3. Shape the mixture as desired.
4. Wrap each sausage in cling film then with aluminum foil.
5. Steam for 30 minutes.
6. Sausages may be later heated up in a pan, in the oven, or on the grill.

Nutritional Values:

Kcal per serve: 287 Fat: 11 g. Protein: 38 g. Carbs: 9 g.

Healthy Green Salad with Mayonnaise

Preparation Time: 20 minutes

Servings: 2

Ingredients:

- 2 tbsp mayonnaise
- 2 small Bok Choy, chopped
- 2 cups watercress
- 2 cups iceberg lettuce, chopped
- 2 cups arugula
- Pepper

Directions:

1. Add all ingredients to the bowl and toss well.
2. Serve and enjoy.

Nutritional Value (Amount per Serving):

Calories 127 Fat 6 g Carbohydrates 14 g Sugar 4 g Protein 8 g Cholesterol 4 mg

Mushroom Lettuce Wraps

Preparation Time: 5minutes

Cooking Time: 16minutes

Serving: 4

Ingredients:

- 2 tbsp butter
- 1 large tomato, sliced
- 4 oz. baby bella mushrooms, sliced
- 1½ lbs. tofu, crumbled
- ¼ tsp black pepper
- 1 iceberg lettuce, leaves extracted
- 1 cup shredded cheddar cheese
- ½ tsp salt

Directions:

1. Put the butter in a skillet and melt over medium heat. Add the mushrooms and sauté until browned and tender, about 6 minutes. Transfer the mushrooms to a plate and set aside.

2. Add the tofu to the skillet, season with salt and black pepper, and cook until brown, about 10 minutes. Turn the heat off.
3. Spoon the tofu and mushrooms into the lettuce leaves, sprinkle with the cheddar cheese, and share the tomato slices on top.
4. Serve the burger immediately.

Nutrition:

Calories:439, Total Fat:31.9 g, Saturated Fat:12.2 g, Total Carbs: 9 g, Dietary Fiber:4g, Sugar:1 g, Protein:36g, Sodium: 574mg

Green Beans, Avocado and Scallions

Preparation time: 10 minutes

Cooking time: 20 minutes

Servings: 4

Ingredients:

- 1 pound green beans, trimmed and halved
- A handful cilantro, chopped
- 1 avocado, peeled, pitted and sliced
- 4 scallions, chopped
- 2 tablespoons olive oil
- Salt and black pepper to the taste
- 1 tablespoon lime juice

Directions:

1. Heat up a pan with the oil over medium heat, add the scallions and sauté for 2 minutes.
2. Add the green beans, lime juice and the other ingredients, toss, cook over medium heat for 18 minutes, divide between plates and serve.

Nutrition:

calories 200, fat 5, fiber 2,3, carbs 1, protein 3

Nutmeg Green Beans

Preparation time: 10 minutes

Cooking time: 30 minutes

Servings: 4

Ingredients:

- 2 tablespoons olive oil
- ½ cup coconut cream
- 1 pound green beans, trimmed and halved
- A pinch of salt and cayenne pepper
- ½ teaspoon onion powder

- 1 teaspoon nutmeg, ground
- ½ teaspoon garlic powder
- 2 tablespoons parsley, chopped

Directions:

1. Heat up a pan with the oil over medium heat, add the green beans, nutmeg and the other ingredients, toss, cook for 30 minutes, divide the mix between plates and serve.

Nutrition:

calories 100, fat 13, fiber 2.3, carbs 5.1, protein 2

Quinoa and Peas

Preparation time: 10 minutes

Cooking time: 30 minutes

Servings: 4

Ingredients:

- 1 tomato, cubed
- 1 yellow onion, chopped

- 1 cup peas
- 1 cup quinoa
- 3 cups vegetable stock
- 1 tablespoon olive oil
- 1 tablespoon cilantro, chopped
- A pinch of salt and black pepper

Directions:

1. Heat up a pot with the oil over medium heat, add the onion, stir and sauté for 5 minutes.
2. Add the quinoa, the stock and the other ingredients, toss, bring to a simmer and cook over medium heat for 25 minutes.
3. Divide everything between plates and serve as a side dish.

Nutrition:

calories 202, fat 3, fiber 3, carbs 11, protein 6

Chocolate Aquafaba Mousse

Preparation Time: 20 mins

Servings: 4-6

Ingredients:

- Fresh raspberries
- 1 tsp. pure vanilla extract
- 15 oz. unsalted chickpeas
- ¼ tsp. tartar cream
- 6 oz. dairy-free dark chocolate
- 2 tbsps. coconut sugar
- ¼ tsp. sea salt

Directions:

1. Chop dark chocolate into coarse bits and place the chocolate into a glass bowl over boiling water on the stovetop or in a double boiler.
2. Melt the chocolate gently, stirring until completely melted.
3. Remove the melted chocolate from the heat and pour the chocolate into a large bowl.
4. Drain the chickpeas, reserving the brine

(aquafaba), and store the chickpeas for another recipe like hummus.

5. Add in the aquafaba along with cream of tartar.
6. Mix on high speed using an electric hand mixer for 7-10 minutes, or until soft peaks begin to form.
7. Add in the salt, vanilla extract, and coconut sugar and beat the mixture until well mixed.
8. Add half of the melted chocolate to the whipped aquafaba and fold it in until incorporated.
9. Fold in the remaining aquafaba until smooth and well combined to form the mousse.
10. Gently spoon the chocolate mousse into glasses, ramekins or small mason jars.
11. Cover with cling film and chill for at least 3 hours.
12. Sprinkle he mousse with raspberries and serve.

Nutrition:

Calories: 280, Fat:13.8 g, Carbs:34.7 g, Protein:3.9 g, Sugars:22 g, Sodium:242 mg

Crispy Radishes

Preparation time: 10 minutes

Cooking time: 20 minutes

Servings: 4

Ingredients:

- 15 radishes, sliced
- Vegetable oil cooking spray
- Salt and ground black pepper, to taste
- 1 tablespoon fresh chives, chopped

Directions:

1. Arrange the radish slices on a lined baking sheet and spray them with cooking oil.
2. Season with salt and pepper, sprinkle with the chives, place in an oven at 375 ºF, and bake for 10 minutes.
3. Flip them and bake for 10 minutes.
4. Serve cold.

Nutrition:

Calories - 30, Fat - 1, Fiber - 0. 4, Carbs - 1, Protein - 0. 1

Radish Soup

Preparation time: 10 minutes

Cooking time: 20 minutes

Servings: 4

Ingredients:

- 2 bunches radishes, cut in quarters
- Salt and ground black pepper, to taste
- 6 cups chicken stock

- 6 garlic cloves, peeled and minced
- 2 stalks celery, chopped
- 3 tablespoons coconut oil
- 1 onion, peeled and chopped

Directions:

1. Heat up a pot with the oil over medium heat, add the onion, celery, and garlic, stir, and cook for 5 minutes.
2. Add the radishes, stock, salt, and pepper, stir, bring to a boil, cover, and simmer for 15 minutes.
3. Divide into soup bowls and serve.

Nutrition:

Calories - 120, Fat - 2, Fiber - 1, Carbs - 3, Protein - 10

Eggplant Stew

Preparation time: 10 minutes

Cooking time: 30 minutes

Servings: 4

Ingredients:

- 5 tomatoes, cored and chopped
- 1 onion, peeled and chopped
- 2 garlic cloves, peeled and chopped
- 1 bunch fresh parsley, chopped
- 1 teaspoon dried oregano
- 2 eggplants, cut into medium-sized chunks
- 2 tablespoons olive oil
- 2 tablespoons capers, chopped
- 12 green olives, pitted and sliced
- Salt and ground black pepper, to taste
- 3 tablespoons herb vinegar

Directions:

1. Heat up a pot with the oil over medium heat, add the eggplant, oregano, salt, and pepper, stir, and cook for 5 minutes.

2. Add the garlic, onion, and parsley, stir, and cook for 4 minutes.
3. Add the capers, olives, vinegar, and tomatoes, stir, and cook for 15 minutes.
4. Add more salt and pepper, if needed, stir, divide into bowls, and serve.

Nutrition:

Calories - 200, Fat - 13, Fiber - 3, Carbs - 5, Protein - 7

Black Bean Soup

Preparation time: 10 minutes

cooking time: 15 minutes

servings: 4

Ingredients

- two 15-ounce cans black beans, drained and rinsed
- 2 tablespoons olive oil
- 1 onion, diced
- 1 green bell pepper, diced
- 1 carrot, peeled and diced
- 4 garlic cloves, minced
- 2 cups vegetable stock
- ¼ teaspoon ground cumin
- 1 teaspoon sea salt
- ¼ cup chopped cilantro, for garnish

Directions

1. In a large soup pot, heat the olive oil over medium-high heat until it shimmers.

2. Add the onion, bell pepper, and carrot and cook until the vegetables soften, about 5 -minutes. Add garlic and cook until it is fragrant, about 30 seconds. Add the black beans, vegetable stock, cumin, and salt. Cook over medium-high heat, occasionally stirring, for about 10 minutes.

3. Remove from the heat. Using a potato masher, mash the beans lightly, leaving some chunks in the soup. For a smoother soup, process in a blender or food processor. Serve hot, garnished with cilantro.

Lime Avocado and Cucumber Soup

Preparation time: 5 minutes

Cooking time: 0 minutes

Servings: 4

Ingredients:

- 2 avocados, pitted, peeled and roughly cubed
- 2 cucumbers, sliced
- Salt and black pepper to the taste

- ¼ teaspoon lemon zest, grated
- 4 cups vegetable stock
- 1 tablespoon white vinegar
- 1 cup scallions, chopped
- 1 tablespoon olive oil
- ¼ cup cilantro, chopped

Directions:

1. In a blender, combine the avocados with the cucumbers and the other ingredients, pulse well, divide into bowls and serve for lunch.

Nutrition:

calories 100, fat 10, fiber 2, carbs 5, protein 8

Lemony Lentil And Rice Soup

Preparation time: 15 minutes

cooking time: 1hour 10 minutes

servings: 6

Ingredients

- 11/4 cups brown lentils, picked over, rinsed, and drained
- 2 tablespoons olive oil
- 1 medium onion, chopped
- 1 medium carrot, cut into 1/4-inch dice
- 1 celery rib, cut into 1/4-inch dice
- ¾ cup long-grain brown rice
- 1 (14.5-ouncecan crushed tomatoes
- 2 cups tomato juice
- 2 bay leaves
- 1/2 teaspoon ground cumin
- 6 cups water
- 1 teaspoon salt
- 1/4 teaspoon freshly ground black pepper
- 1 tablespoon fresh lemon juice
- 2 tablespoons minced fresh parsley

Directions

1. In a large soup pot, heat the oil over medium heat. Add the onion, carrot, and celery. Cover and cook until tender, about 10 minutes.

2. Add the lentils, rice, tomatoes, tomato juice, bay leaves, cumin, water, salt, and pepper. Bring to a boil, then reduce heat to medium low, and simmer, uncovered, until lentils and rice are tender, about 1 hour.

3. Just before serving, remove and discard the bay leaves, and stir in the lemon juice and parsley. Taste, adjusting seasonings if necessary, and serve.

Three Bean Soup

Preparation Time: 5 Minutes

Cooking Time: 52 Minutes

Servings:4 To 6

Ingredients

- 1 medium onion, chopped
- 1 medium carrot, chopped
- 2 tablespoons olive oil
- 1 cup chopped celery
- 2 garlic cloves, minced
- 1 (14.5-ounce) can diced tomatoes, drained
- 11/2 cups cooked or 1 (15.5-ounce) can dark red kidney beans, drained and rinsed
- 11/2 cups cooked or 1 (15.5-ounce) can black beans, drained and rinsed
- 11/2 cups cooked or 1 (15.5-ounce) can navy or other white beans, drained and rinsed
- 4 cups vegetable broth, homemade (see Light Vegetable Broth) or store-bought, or water
- 1 tablespoon soy sauce
- 1 teaspoon dried thyme

- 1 bay leaf
- Salt and freshly ground black pepper
- 2 tablespoons chopped fresh parsley

Directions

1. In a large soup pot, heat the oil over medium heat. Add the onion, carrot, celery, and garlic. Cover and cook until softened, about 7 minutes. Uncover, and stir in the tomatoes, all the beans, and the broth. Add the soy sauce, thyme, and bay leaf and season with salt and pepper to taste. Bring to a boil, then reduce heat to low and simmer until the vegetables are tender, about 45 minutes.
2. Remove the bay leaf and discard before serving. Add the parsley and serve.

Zucchini Risotto

Preparation time: 10 minutes

Cooking time: 30 minutes

Servings: 4

Ingredients:

- ½ cup shallots, chopped
- 3 garlic cloves, minced
- 2 tablespoons olive oil
- 2 cups cauliflower rice

- ½ cup white mushrooms, chopped
- 1 cup zucchinis, cubed
- 2 cups veggie stock
- ½ teaspoon coriander, ground
- A pinch of salt and black pepper
- ¼ teaspoon oregano, dried
- 2 tablespoons parsley, chopped

Directions:

1. Heat up a pan with the oil over medium heat, add the shallots, garlic, mushrooms, coriander and oregano, stir and sauté for 10 minutes.
2. Add the cauliflower rice and the other ingredients, toss, cook for 20 minutes more, divide between plates and serve.

Nutrition:

calories 231, fat 5, fiber 3, carbs 9, protein 12

Tempeh Alfredo Squash Spaghetti

Preparation Time: 1 hour and 20 minutes

Serving: 4

Ingredients:

For the pasta:

- 2 medium spaghetti squashes, halved
- 2 tbsp olive oil

For the sauce:

- 2 tbsp butter
- 1 lb tempeh, crumbled
- ½ tsp garlic powder
- A pinch of nutmeg
- 1/3 cup finely grated parmesan cheese
- Salt and black pepper to taste
- 1 tsp arrowroot starch
- 1 ½ cups coconut cream
- 1/3 cup finely grated tempeh mozzarella cheese

Directions:

1. Preheat the oven to 375 °F and line a baking dish with foil. Set aside.

2. Season the squash with olive oil, salt, and black pepper. Place the squash on the baking dish, open side up and roast for 45 to 50 minutes until the squash is tender.

3. When ready, remove the squash from the oven, allow cooling and use two forks to shred the inner part of the noodles. Set aside.

4. Melt the butter in a medium pot, add the tempeh, garlic powder, salt, and black pepper, cook until brown, 10 minutes.

5. Stir in the arrowroot starch, coconut cream, and nutmeg. Cook until the sauce thickens, 2 to 3 minutes.

6. Spoon the sauce into the squashes and cover with the parmesan and mozzarella cheeses.

7. Place under the oven's broiler and cook until the cheeses melt and golden brown, 2 to 3 minutes.

8. Remove from the oven and serve warm.

Nutrition:

Calories:865, Total Fat:80.2g, Saturated Fat:56.8g, Total Carbs: 19g, Dietary Fiber:5g, Sugar: 5g, Protein: 28g, Sodium: 1775mg

Classic Tempeh Lasagna

Preparation Time: 70 minutes

Serving: 4

Ingredients:

For the lasagna noodles:

- 4 oz dairy- free cream cheese, room temperature
- 1 tsp dried Italian seasoning
- 1 ½ cup grated mozzarella cheese
- 2 large eggs, cracked into a bowl

For the lasagna filling:

- 1 lb tempeh
- 1 medium white onion, chopped
- 1 tsp Italian seasoning
- 1 cup sugar-free marinara sauce
- 6 tbsp vegan ricotta cheese
- ½ cup grated mozzarella cheese
- Salt and black pepper to taste
- ½ cup grated parmesan cheese

Directions:

For the lasagna noodles:

1. Preheat the oven to 350 ^{0}F and line a 9 x 13 – inch baking sheet with parchment paper.
2. In a food processor or blender, add the dairy-free cream cheese, mozzarella cheese, Italian seasoning, and eggs. Blend until well mixed.
3. Pour the cheese mixture on the baking sheet and spread across the pan.
4. Bake in the middle layer of the oven until set and firm to touch, 20 minutes.
5. Remove the cheese pasta and set aside to cool while you make the lasagna sauce.

For the lasagna sauce:

6. In a large skillet, combine the tempeh, onion and cook until brown, 5 minutes. Season with the Italian seasoning, salt, and black pepper. Cook further for 1 minute and mix in the marinara sauce. Simmer for 3 minutes. Turn the heat off.
7. Evenly cut the lasagna pasta into thirds making sure it fits into your baking sheet.
8. Spread a layer of the tempeh mixture in the baking sheet and make a first single layer on

the tempeh mixture.

9. Spread a third of the remaining tempeh mixture on the pasta, top with a third each of the vegan ricotta cheese, mozzarella cheese, and parmesan cheese. Repeat the layering two more times using the remaining Ingredients in the same quantities.

10. Bake in the oven until the cheese melts and is bubbly with the sauce, 20 minutes.

11. Remove the lasagna, allow cooling for 2 minutes and dish onto serving plates. Serve warm

Nutrition:

Calories:435, Total Fat:38.3g, Saturated Fat:1.2g, Total Carbs: 4 g, Dietary Fiber:1g, Sugar: 2g, Protein21: g, Sodium: 388mg

Mango And Snow Pea Salad

Preparation time: 15 minutes

cooking time: 0 minutes

servings: 4

Ingredients

- 1/2 teaspoon minced garlic
- 1/2 teaspoon grated fresh ginger
- 1 medium cucumber, peeled, halved lengthwise, and seeded
- 1/4 cup creamy peanut butter
- 2 cups snow peas, trimmed and lightly blanched
- 2 ripe mangos, peeled, pitted, cut into 1/2-inch dice
- 1 tablespoon plus 1 teaspoon light brown sugar
- 1/4 teaspoon crushed red pepper
- 3 tablespoons rice vinegar
- 3 tablespoons water
- 1 tablespoon soy sauce
- 1 large carrot, shredded
- 3 cups shredded romaine lettuce
- 1/2 cup chopped unsalted roasted peanuts, for garnish

Directions

1. In a small bowl, combine the garlic, ginger, peanut butter, sugar, and crushed red pepper. Stir in the vinegar, water, and soy sauce. Taste, adjusting seasonings, if necessary, and set aside.

2. Cut the snow peas diagonally into a thin matchsticks and place in a large bowl. Add the mangos and carrot. Cut the cucumber into 1/4-inch slices and add to the bowl.

3. Pour the dressing onto the salad and toss gently to combine. Spoon the salad onto a bed of shredded lettuce, sprinkle with peanuts, and serve.

Cobb Salad with Portobello Bacon

Preparation Time: 15 Minutes

Cooking Time: 0 Minutes

Servings:4

Ingredients

- 2 heads romaine lettuce, finely chopped
- 1 pint cherry tomatoes, halved
- 1 avocado, peeled, pitted, and diced

- Portobello Bacon or store-bought vegan bacon
- 1 cup frozen (and thawed) or fresh corn kernels
- 1 large cucumber, peeled and diced
- 4 scallions, thinly sliced
- Unhidden Valley Ranch Dressing or store-bought vegan ranch dressing

Directions

1. Scatter a layer of romaine in the bottom of each of 4 salad bowls. With the following ingredients, create lines that cross the top of the romaine, in this order: tomatoes, avocado, corn, cucumber, and portobello bacon.
2. Sprinkle with the scallions and drizzle with ranch dressing.

Tuscan White Bean Salad

Preparation time: 10 minutes • marinating time: 30 minutes •

servings: 2

Ingredients

For the dressing

- 1 tablespoon olive oil
- 2 tablespoons balsamic vinegar
- 1 tablespoon fresh rosemary, chopped, or 1 teaspoon dried
- 1 tablespoon fresh oregano, chopped, or 1 teaspoon dried
- 1 teaspoon minced fresh chives, or scallions
- 1 garlic clove, pressed or minced
- Pinch sea salt

For the salad

- 1 zucchini, diced
- 1 (14-ouncecan cannellini beans, drained and rinsed, or 1½ cups cooked
- 6 mushrooms, thinly sliced
- 2 carrots, diced

- 2 tablespoons fresh basil, chopped

Directions

1. Make the dressing by whisking all the dressing ingredients together in a large bowl.
2. Toss all the salad ingredients with the dressing. For the best flavor, put the salad in a sealed container, shake it vigorously, and leave to marinate 15 to 30 minutes.

Nutrition

Calories: 360; Total fat: 8g; Carbs: 68g; Fiber: 15g; Protein: 18g

Cucumber And Onion Quinoa Salad

Preparation time: 15 minutes

cooking time: 20 minutes

servings: 4

Ingredients

- 1½ cups dry quinoa, rinsed and drained
- 2¼ cups water
- ⅓ cup white wine vinegar
- 2 tablespoons extra-virgin olive oil
- 1 tablespoon chopped fresh dill
- 1½ teaspoons vegan sugar
- ¼ teaspoon freshly ground black pepper
- 2 cups sliced sweet onions
- 2 cups diced cucumber
- 2 pinches salt
- 4 cups shredded lettuce

Directions

1. In a medium pot, combine the quinoa and water. Bring to a boil.

2. Cover, reduce the heat to medium-low, and simmer for 15 to 20 minutes, until the water is absorbed. Remove from the stove and let stand for 5 minutes. Fluff with a fork and set aside.
3. Meanwhile, in a small bowl, mix the vinegar, olive oil, dill, sugar, salt, and pepper. Set aside. Into each of 4 wide-mouth jars, add 2 tablespoons of dressing, ½ cup of onions, ½ cup of cucumber, 1 cup of cooked quinoa, and 1 cup of shredded lettuce. Seal the lids tightly.

Nutrition:

Calories: 369; Fat: 11g; Protein: 10g; Carbohydrates: 58g; Fiber: 6g; Sugar: 12g; Sodium: 88mg

Giardiniera

Preparation time: 15 minutes

cooking time: 0 minutes

servings: 6

Ingredients

- 1 medium carrot, cut into 1/4-inch rounds
- 1 medium red bell pepper, cut into 1/2-inch dice
- 1 cup small cauliflower florets
- 2 celery ribs, finely chopped
- 1/2 cup chopped onion
- 1/4 cup sliced pimiento-stuffed green olives
- 1 garlic clove, minced
- 1/2 teaspoon sugar (optional)
- 2 tablespoons salt (optional)
- 1/2 teaspoon crushed red pepper
- 1/4 teaspoon freshly ground black pepper
- 3 tablespoons white wine vinegar
- 1/3 cup olive oil

Directions

1. In a large bowl, combine the carrot, bell pepper, cauliflower, celery, and onion. Stir in the salt and add enough cold water to cover. Tightly cover the bowl and refrigerate for 4 to 6 hours.

2. Drain and rinse the vegetables and place them in a large bowl. Add the olives and set them aside.

3. In a small bowl, combine the garlic, sugar, crushed red pepper, black pepper, vinegar, and oil, and mix well. Pour the dressing over the vegetables and toss gently to combine. Cover and refrigerate overnight before serving.

Summer Berries With Fresh Mint

Preparation Time: 15 Minutes

Cooking Time: 0 Minutes

Servings:4 To 6

Ingredients

- 2 tablespoons fresh orange or pineapple juice
- 2 cups pitted fresh cherries
- 1 cup fresh blueberries
- 1 tablespoon fresh lime juice
- 1 tablespoon agave nectar
- 2 teaspoons minced fresh mint
- 1 cup fresh strawberries, hulled and halved
- 1/2 cup fresh blackberries or raspberries

Directions

1. In a small bowl, combine the orange juice, lime juice, agave nectar, and mint. Set aside.
2. In a large bowl, combine the cherries, blueberries, strawberries, and blackberries. Add the dressing and toss gently to combine. Serve immediately.

Tamari Toasted Almonds

Preparation time: 2 minutes

cooking time: 8 minutes

servings: ½ cup

Ingredients

- ½ cup raw almonds, or sunflower seeds
- 2 tablespoons tamari, or soy sauce
- 1 teaspoon toasted sesame oil

Directions

1. Heat a dry skillet to medium-high heat, then add the almonds, stirring very frequently to keep them from burning. Once the almonds are toasted, 7 to 8 minutes for almonds, or 3 to 4 minutes for sunflower seeds, pour the tamari and sesame oil into the hot skillet and stir to coat.

2. You can turn off the heat, and as the almonds cool the tamari mixture will stick to and dry on the nuts.

Nutrition (1 tablespoon)

Calories: 89; Total fat: 8g; Carbs: 3g; Fiber: 2g; Protein: 4g

Cabbage Sticks

Preparation time: 10 minutes

Cooking time: 30 minutes

Servings: 4

Ingredients:

- 1 pound cabbage, leaves separated and cut into thick strips
- 1 teaspoon ginger, grated
- 1 tablespoon olive oil
- 1 tablespoon balsamic vinegar
- 1 teaspoon hot paprika
- A pinch of salt and black pepper

Directions:

1. Spread the cabbage strips on a baking sheet lined with parchment paper, add the oil, the vinegar and the other ingredients, toss and cook at 400 degrees F for 30 minutes.
2. Divide the cabbage strips into bowls and serve as a snack.

Nutrition:

calories 300, fat 4, fiber 7, carbs 18, protein 6

Almond and Pine Nuts Spread

Preparation time: 10 minutes

Cooking time: 15 minutes

Servings: 8

Ingredients:

- 1 cup coconut cream
- ½ cup almonds, chopped
- 2 tablespoons pine nuts, toasted

- 1 teaspoon chili powder
- 1 tablespoon olive oil
- 1 teaspoon sage, ground
- A pinch of salt and black pepper

Directions:

1. In a pot, combine the almonds with the pine nuts, cream and the other ingredients, stir, cook over medium heat for 15 minutes and transfer to a blender.
2. Pulse well, divide into bowls and serve as a party spread.

Nutrition:

calories 112, fat 5, fiber 2, carbs 8, protein 10

Mushroom Falafel

Preparation time: 10 minutes

Cooking time: 12 minutes

Servings: 6

Ingredients:

- 1 cup mushrooms, chopped
- 1 bunch parsley leaves
- 4 scallions, hopped
- 5 garlic cloves, minced
- 1 teaspoon coriander, ground
- A pinch of salt and black pepper
- ¼ teaspoon baking soda
- 1 teaspoon lemon juice
- 3 tablespoons almond flour
- 2 tablespoons avocado oil

Directions:

1. In your food processor, combine the mushrooms with the parsley and the other ingredients except the flour and the oil and pulse well.

2. Transfer the mix to a bowl, add the flour, stir well, shape medium balls out of this mix and flatten them a bit.
3. Heat up a pan with the over medium-high heat, add the falafels, cook them for 6 minutes on each side, drain excess grease using paper towels, arrange them on a platter and serve as an appetizer.

Nutrition:

calories 55, fat 3.5, fiber 1.5, carbs 4.5, protein 2.3

Baked Hot Spicy Cashews Snack

Preparation Time: 20 minutes

Cooking Time: 35 minutes

Servings: 8

Ingredients:

- 2½ c. raw cashews
- ½ tsp. turmeric powder
- 1/3 c. olive oil
- 1 tsp. garlic powder
- 3 c. hot pepper sauce

Directions:

1. In a mixing bowl, mix hot pepper sauce, oil and stir in the turmeric and garlic powder.
2. Add the cashews to the bowl and completely coat with hot pepper sauce mixture.
3. Soak cashews in the hot sauce mixture for several hours.
4. Preheat oven to 325 ⁰F.
5. Spread the cashews onto a baking sheet and bake for 35-35 minutes.
6. Allow cool and serve.

Nutrition:

Calories: 41, Fat: 29.01g, Carbs: 9.6g, Protein: 6.71g

Cinnamon Bun Balls

Preparation Time: 15 minutes

Cooking Time: 0 minute

Servings: 10

Ingredients:

- 1/2 cup whole walnuts
- 5 medjool dates, pitted
- 1 tablespoon chopped walnuts
- 3 tablespoons ground cinnamon
- 1 teaspoon ground cardamom

Directions:

1. Place all the ingredients in a food processor, except for one tablespoon walnuts, and then process until smooth.
2. Shape the mixture into ten balls, then roll them into chopped walnuts and serve.

Nutrition:

Calories:62 Cal, Fat: 4.5 g, Carbs: 5.8 g, Protein: 1.2 g, Fiber: 2 g

Kale Hummus

Preparation Time: 5 minutes

Cooking Time: 0 minute

Servings: 4

Ingredients:

- 2 cups cooked chickpeas
- 5 cloves of garlic, peeled
- 4 cups kale, torn into pieces

- 1/3 cup lemon juice
- 1/4 cup olive oil
- 1/4 cup tahini
- 1 teaspoon of sea salt

Directions:

1. Place all the ingredients in a bowl and pulse for 2 minutes until smooth.
2. Tip the hummus in a bowl, drizzle with oil, and then serve.

Nutrition:

Calories: 173 Cal, Fat: 10 g, Carbs: 14 g, Protein: 6 g, Fiber: 5 g

Banana-Nut Bread Bars

Preparation time: 5 minutes

cooking time: 30 minutes

servings: 9 bars

Ingredients

- Nonstick cooking spray (optional
- ½ teaspoon vanilla extract
- 2 large ripe bananas
- 1 tablespoon maple syrup
- 2 cups old-fashioned rolled oats
- ½ teaspoons salt
- ¼ cup chopped walnuts

Directions

1. Preheat the oven to 350ºF. Lightly coat a 9-by-9-inch baking pan with nonstick cooking spray (if usingor line with parchment paper for oil-free baking.

2. In a medium bowl, mash the bananas with a fork. Add the maple syrup and vanilla extract and mix well. Add the oats, salt, and walnuts, mixing well.

3. Transfer the batter to the baking pan and bake for 25 to 30 minutes, until the top is crispy. Cool completely before slicing into 9 bars. Transfer to an airtight storage container or a large plastic bag.

Nutrition (1 bar):

Calories: 73; Fat: 1g; Protein: 2g; Carbohydrates: 15g; Fiber: 2g; Sugar: 5g; Sodium: 129mg

Ginger-Spice Brownies

Preparation time: 5 minutes

cooking time: 35 minutes

servings: 12 brownies

Ingredients

- 1¾ cups whole-grain flour
- 1 teaspoon baking powder
- 1 teaspoon baking soda
- 1 tablespoon ground ginger
- 1/2 teaspoon ground cinnamon
- 1/2 cup vegan semisweet chocolate chips
- 1/2 teaspoon ground allspice
- 3 tablespoons unsweetened cocoa powder
- 1/2 cup chopped walnuts
- 1/4 cup canola oil
- 1/2 cup dark molasses
- 1/2 teaspoon salt
- 1/2 cup water
- 1/3 cup light brown sugar
- 2 teaspoons grated fresh ginger

Directions

1. Preheat the oven to 350 °F. Grease an 8-inch square baking pan and set aside. In a large bowl, combine the flour, baking powder, baking soda, salt, ground ginger, cinnamon, allspice, and cocoa. Stir in the chocolate chips and walnuts and set aside.

2. In medium bowl, combine the oil, molasses, water, sugar, and fresh ginger and mix well.

3. Pour the wet Ingredients into the dry Ingredients and mix well.

4. Scrape the dough into the prepared baking pan. The dough will be sticky, so wet your hands to press it evenly into the pan. Bake until a toothpick inserted in the center comes out clean, 30 to 35 minutes. Cool on a wire rack 30 minutes before cutting. Store in an airtight container.

Popovers

Preparation Time: 5 mins

Servings: 6

Ingredients:

- 1 c. fat-free milk
- 4 egg whites
- 1 c. All-purpose flour
- ¼ tsp. salt

Directions:

1. Preheat your oven to 425 ^{0}F.
2. Coat a six cup metal or glass muffin mold with cooking spray and heat the mold in the oven for two minutes.
3. In a bowl, add the flour, milk, salt, and egg whites. Use a mixer to beat until it's smooth.
4. Fill the heated molds two-thirds of the way full.
5. Bake until the muffins are golden brown and puffy, around half an hour. Serve.

Nutrition:

Calories: 101, Fat:0 g, Carbs:18 g, Protein:6 g, Sugars:2 g, Sodium:125 mg

Watermelon Mousse

Preparation time: 10 minutes

Cooking time: 0 minutes

Servings: 4

Ingredients:

- 1 cup coconut cream
- 1 tablespoon lemon juice
- 2 cups watermelon, peeled and cubed
- 1 tablespoon stevia

Directions:

1. In a blender, combine the watermelon with the cream, the lemon juice and stevia, pulse well, divide into bowls and serve cold.

Nutrition:

calories 332, fat 31.4, fiber 0.5, carbs 9.2, protein 5.5

Apple & Walnut Cake.

Preparation Time: 20 Minutes

Servings: 6

Ingredients:

- 1¾ cups unbleached all-purpose flour
- 1 tablespoon freshly squeezed lemon juice
- 1 teaspoon pure vanilla extract
- 1½ teaspoons ground cinnamon
- 1 cup unsweetened applesauce
- ⅔ cup packed light brown sugar
- ½ cup chopped walnuts
- ¼ cup vegetable oil
- 1 teaspoon baking powder
- ½ teaspoon baking soda
- ½ teaspoon salt
- ¼ teaspoon ground allspice
- ¼ teaspoon ground nutmeg
- ⅛ teaspoon ground cloves

Directions:

1. Lightly oil a baking tray that will fit in the steamer basket of your Cooker.
2. In a bowl, combine the flour, baking powder, baking soda, sugar, cinnamon, allspice, nutmeg, cloves, and salt.
3. In another bowl combine the applesauce, oil, vanilla, and lemon juice.
4. Stir the wet mixture into the dry mixture slowly until they form a smooth mix.
5. Fold in the walnuts.
6. Pour the batter into your baking tray and put the tray in your steamer basket.
7. Pour the minimum amount of water into the base of your Cooker and lower the steamer basket.
8. Seal and cook on Steam for 12 minutes.
9. Release the pressure quickly and set to one side to cool a little.

Gluten-Free Nutella Brownie Trifle

Preparation time: 60 minutes

Ingredients:

For the brownies:

- 6 Oz. hazelnuts
- ½ cup almonds
- ½ cup cashews
- 1 cup medjool dates, pitted
- ½ tsp. vanilla extract
- 2 tbsp. cacao powder
- 2 tbsp. hazelnut butter
- 1 tbsp. maple syrup or honey, to taste

For the frosting:

- ½ tsp. vanilla
- ½ cup avocado, fresh crushed
- 1 ½ tbsp. coconut oil
- 2tbsp. coconut maple syrup
- 1 tbsp. cacao
- 1 tbsp. nut butter

Directions:

1. You will need some baking paper for lining the baking tray.
2. Dry the hazelnuts and almonds in a frying pan until toasted.
3. Add ¾ of all the nuts with the almonds into the food processor until they are broken to chunks.
4. Add the dates and process again, then all the rest ingredients until you have a sticky mass.
5. Pour it onto the baking tray lined with paper. Press the crumbly mixture you made with your fingers until the top of it is even. Place into the fridge while you are cooking the glaze.
6. For the glaze you will have to mix well all the ingredients in a bowl or process them all in a food processor until well combined. It should be smooth and creamy.
7. Remove your brownie from a fridge add the frosting on top spreading it evenly.
8. Top the brownie with the remaining nuts and place again into the fridge until you have it served.

Keto Vegan Pumpkin Mousse

Preparation time: 15 minutes

Ingredients:

- 15 oz. firm Tofu
- 15 oz. organic Pumpkin
- ½ tsp. Ginger
- 1 tbsp. Cinnamon
- Stevia for sweetening

Directions:

1. Mix all the ingredients in a blender until smooth. Taste and add more stevia for sweetening.

Lime Berries Stew

Preparation time: 10 minutes

Cooking time: 20 minutes

Servings: 6

Ingredients:

- Zest of 1 lime, grated
- 1 pint strawberries, halved
- 2 cups water
- Juice of 1 lime
- 2 tablespoons stevia

Directions:

1. In a pan, combine the strawberries with the lime juice, the water and stevia, toss, bring to a simmer and cook over medium heat for 20 minutes.
2. Divide the stew into bowls and serve cold.

Nutrition:

calories 172, fat 7, fiber 3.4, carbs 8, protein 2.3

Lemon Mousse

Preparation Time: 10 minutes

Cooking Time: 0 minute

Servings: 2

Ingredients:

- 14 oz coconut milk
- 1/2 tsp lemon extract
- 12 drops liquid stevia
- 1/4 tsp turmeric

Directions:

1. Place coconut milk can in the refrigerator for overnight. Scoop out thick cream into a mixing bowl.
2. Add remaining ingredients to the bowl and whip using a hand mixer until smooth.
3. Transfer mousse mixture to a zip-lock bag and pipe into small serving glasses. Place in refrigerator.
4. Serve chilled and enjoy.

Nutritions:

Calories 444, Fat 45.7g, Carbohydrates 10g, Sugar 6g, Protein 4.4g, Cholesterol 0mg

NOTE

CPSIA information can be obtained
at www.ICGtesting.com
Printed in the USA
BVHW040712230321
603253BV00007B/222